Avoiding Karma

A Guide to Assuring Personal Ascension

by

Guy Steven Needler

For permission, serialization, condensation, adaptions, or for our catalog of other publications, write to Ozark Mountain Publishing, Inc., P.O. box 754, Huntsville, AR 72740, ATTN: Permissions Department.

Library of Congress Cataloging-in-Publication Data

Needler, Guy Steven -1961

Avoiding Karma: A Guide to Assuring Personal Ascension by Guy Steven Needler

Methods to avoid creating karma to assist one's own spiritual development.

1. Karma 2. Spiritual Growth 3. Metaphysics

1. Needler, Guy Steven, 1961 II. Karma III. Title

Library of Congress Catalog Card Number: 2014933819

ISBN: 9781886940468

Cover Design: enki3d.com

Book set in: Times New Roman, Andalus

Book Design: Tab Pillar

Published by:

PO Box 754

Huntsville, AR 72740

800-935-0045 or 479-738-2348 fax: 479-738-2448

WWW.OZARKMT.COM

Printed in the United States of America

For my dear wife

Anne Elizabeth Milner

Now "Ascended"

(10th April 1957 – 24th December 2012)

Table of Contents

Introduction

The information within this book, given to me by the Source Entity, is specifically designed to make us, dear readers, think, and thus, to make us change our ways, to recognize who and what we truly are, and to come out of our incarnate slumber and ascend.

However, to do this we need to be vigilant.

This is not a large book; it was not meant to be large. It has fewer than 120 pages and could be easily read in a day. However, I urge you not to do so. I ask you to read each excerpt in isolation and work with it to the very best of your ability. Absorb that which is presented to you and become free of the constraints of the physical, shrugging off karma and ascending in the process. Read a maximum of two excerpts a week and create a personal commitment to follow that which is presented. Or, better still, read one a week and be robust in your application of the advice. Observe your performance and make corrections where necessary, doing so with love in your heart and leading by example.

Love transcends karma; it is all about the multiverse.

Karma is only a function of the physical universe, and our true energetic selves, when attracted to the lower frequencies associated with the physical universe, are linked to it. Hence the need to return to it to break the link, to break the karmic cycle. Once the link with the physical is broken, the need to incarnate is no longer necessary, and the true energetic self can ascend the frequencies and evolve in the process without needing to experience ever again those lower frequencies associated with the physical universe.

Self-Love and the love of others is, therefore, a key to ascension, and when one has finished this book, one will be "In Love," "In Ascension"—avoiding karma in the process.

Guy Steven Needler

1st February 2013

Reacting to Taunts

The first stage in avoiding karma is not to react to the taunts and jibes of those we interface with but instead for us to see them as beings on an evolutionary path as we are. Looking beneath the words and actions of the accuser for the greater meaning, we must be the tolerant and benevolent observer, understanding the experience of the lessons we are offered by them and reacting with compassion and thanks. Thus, we evolve in the process.

Beware of the Digital Reality

Karma is a function of attraction to the physical and also works in/with our interfacing with the digital reality because it is a function of the physical. As such, it is also a potential addiction, serving to anchor us to the physical.

Owning Only What We Need

We are reminded to look at what we need in life versus what we want in life. If our need is less than our want, then we have a potential for accruing the lower frequencies or karma associated with the attraction to ownership of physical belongings. This is a function of karma, which is never satisfied, for the more we have, the more we seem to want.

Loving Our Enemies; for We Are One

To love our enemies is to love ourselves, for our enemies are our "selves." Recognition of the fact that we are all "one" and one with God removes the need to identify others as our enemies. How can people truly be our enemies when they are just another part of us?! Recognition of this reality and taking action, based upon it, is a most powerful way of avoiding karma.

Being of Service

We are here to be of service to those who need help and do so in a selfless way that does not demand reward. Being of service in general creates positive karma (attraction to the higher frequencies), but we must be careful not to get into the mindset that suggests that we will be rewarded at some time, for this creates negative karma (attraction to the lower frequencies).

Defining Our Motivation

Standing back and considering the motivation behind our actions is necessary. Are we motivated based upon need or greed? Service or selfishness? Any actions that are based upon physical motivations are attractions to negative karma.

Avoiding Gossip

When we avoid being pulled into gossip or starting gossip, we are using good judgment. Gossip is the most effective way to accrue the negative karma experienced by mankind.

Gossip is a particularly insidious pastime as it drags us into the lower frequency energies of another, effectively boosting that person's energy. As more people join in the "gossip," the leader of the gossip becomes the center of a collective that is created by energies that are usually focused upon the derision of another. This is the creation of a collective and its synergetic effects for the wrong reason. This effectively links us as members of the collective to an energy sink that creates an "overlay" mentality that circumvents our personal [mentality/thinking] and destroys our free will.

The antidote is for us to not get involved in gossip by finely tuning our "observer selves"—an observational tool that allows us to look from the perspective of an outsider of such discussions. If we see ourselves as already engaged in gossip, it is time for us to say we have no further comment and then walk away.

Shunning Judgment

Judgment, both individual and collective, is a function of gossip and, therefore, provides a clear and direct path to low frequency existence, creating a downward spiral, frequency-wise.

Judgment is, therefore, something that we should never enter into, for it is a function of personalized perception of the processes that led to a certain position, but not the actual ones that lead to "fact" and not "judgment."

Choosing Our Friends with Care

Being of good cheer and surrounding ourselves with like-minded individuals whilst incarnate is wise. We should avoid those who drag us down by enticing us to be part of lower frequency actions.

Colluding to Gain False Friends

A more insidious form of karma can be observed in the need to collude. Collusion is that which we do when we seek favor from others to be part of "the" team, "the" group, or to be with someone of influence whose association, we think, will benefit us in some social, business or egotistical way, thus, giving us the "upper hand."

The need to collude is, therefore, based upon physical desires and, as such, attracts those lower frequencies associated with the more subtle aspects of physical existence.

Seeking Favors, a Form of Collusion

Seeking favor with another is a form of collusion and results in an expectation of personal benefit from the favor. When we seek favor, we are ALWAYS looking for some sort of reward as a result of the favor, which when not given, results in our being disappointed, then thinking negatively, and having feelings of betrayal. When we require and receive a favor, we are in "favor debt" to the person giving us the favor. This results in negative anticipation of what the requested favor might be and whether we can support such a request to the expectations of the requester. As a result, the returned favor is always greater than that initially given.

We should, therefore, not seek favors but should give freely as a gift that which is requested. Thus, we should expect nothing in return, except God's love because the reward of recognition of such a potential karmic loop is now broken.

Being Aware of Automatic Addictions

It is important for us to stand back and look at what we do on a daily and automatic basis.

How much of what we do is necessary for us to survive? How much is an addiction to physical "pleasure" that is based upon an automated action/response? If we give up our addictions, we will lose automatically generated karma.

Noticing Minor Addictions

Being aware of minor addictions is necessary, especially the ones that we may consider to be not an addiction but more of a preference. Addictions of any type are a constant link to the low frequencies. Minor addictions are insidious and invisible to all but the most vigilant of truth seekers.

Being Addicted to Sex

Our engaging in sex for procreation is both a necessity and a delight. However, engaging in sex for recreation can lead us down the path of addiction to the physical sensation associated with sex, which is a low frequency function.

Discerning Fears

When we look at our fears, it is important to notice where they are anchored. Are they about work, relationships, possessions, appearance, personal credibility or money? Any of these are fears that are based in the physical environment and are nothing we would pay any attention to in the energetic. If we don't pay attention to these or any other types of fear in the energetic, then why should we pay attention to them whilst incarnate, for fear is a product of being in the lower frequencies associated with incarnate existence.

Choosing Love

Love is the antidote to karma, so we must

- Love God;
- Love our neighbors;
- Love our enemies.
- Love our partners/our wives;
- Love ourselves;
- Love our mistakes;
- Love our successes;
- Love our current experiences;
- Love our planet;
- Love our teachers; and
- Love that which presents its "self" to offer us experience, learning and evolution.

If we love all of these things in an unreserved way, we will surely avoid karma for life!

Being Calm

Being of a calm demeanor and entering into everything we do in a calm and collected way, irrespective of the environment in which we find ourselves is so important. When we are confronted with adverse conditions, it is easy for us to become part of those conditions and be drawn into the lower frequencies that created them.

By staying calm, we are able to rise above the drama, remain unaffected, and achieve an efficient response whilst staying within the high frequencies. In this way we can and do work with the physical whilst being "in" the physical without being "of" the physical. Thus, calmness is a state of mind that deflects the opportunity for gaining karmic content through spontaneous response.

Remaining in calmness in all situations makes our "observer self" come into play. This ensures that the bigger picture is taken into account and allows us to respond in a respectful, thoughtful and knowledgeable way. Thus, we must strive to maintain calmness at all times.

Thinking Before Responding

It is good practice the moment we wake up in the morning to think about what we can do to avoid attraction to the low frequency energies we call karma.

Consciously avoiding karma takes significant practice until it is achieved on an automatic basis. If we think about everything we are doing or are about to do with a view toward the possibility of accruing karma and then think about how we can avoid it, we will make inroads into awareness of how to make this practice a regular part of our lives.

Once we have established "karma-safe" responses, then we can do, say and react in those ways in preference to our former instantaneous and "off the cuff" responses and reactions. Once we get used to reacting and working in a karma-safe way, we will notice over a period of time that we are getting "lighter". This is the proof that we are attracting higher frequency energies, accruing positive karma and accelerating our evolutionary process.

Communing with God to Create Heaven

When we are in the energetic, we are totally free and have instant communication with our peers and our Creator. We have no constraints and are not encumbered by a physical body, for then we are in our normal high frequency, high dimensional environment.

When we are incarnate, we are trapped in extremely limited and slow bodies that decay, cut off our communication with our energetic peers and our Creator, and, are subject to pain, discomfort, illness and disease. In comparison to our normal energetic environment, it is hell. We can, however, alleviate the level of hellish experience by endeavoring to commune with the rest of us that is still in the energetic with our Creator, our Source Entity, our God.

By communing with God and our true selves whilst incarnate, as well as living in a way that does not attract the lower frequencies associated with the physical (karma), we can experience in some limited way that which we experience whilst in the energetic—what we may refer to as "heaven." We can, therefore, through correct living and dedicated meditation, make "heaven" on Earth. To not do so and to go against this way of life, we can and do make our own hell on Earth!

Being Happy and Kind

It is easy to always smile when we remember our knowledge of the greater reality. Saying "Good morning" to others, always replying in a positive manner, opening the door for the person behind us, and letting the other person have the parking spot or pull out into the queue before us is a natural part of that remembrance. Why wouldn't we provide help to those who need it, assist those in need of an escort across the road, and make a habit of being kind and doing "good" things?

These small things increase our frequencies, as well as the frequencies of those around us. In doing these small things, we decrease our opportunities of accruing the lower frequencies associated with karma, not only for us but everyone else. This in itself is a great kindness and an even greater service as it increases joy in the world.

Avoiding Karma

Addressing Our Responsibilities

Just because we are seekers of the truth, know the greater reality, and commune with God on a daily basis, it doesn't mean that we are able ignore our roles and responsibilities whilst in the physical. We planned these responsibilities as part of our experiences, our learning, and our evolution. To ignore them means our incarnation is meaningless and will result in karma with the need for us to incarnate again to fulfill the experiences set out in our previous plan.

We are here to know the greater reality, to know God and to deliver our earthly duties with skill and perfection, thus avoiding karma in the process.

Allowing Others to Have Their Beliefs

We must never assume that as spiritual individuals devoted to knowing the greater reality; we can convert someone else who is not yet ready to know the truth.

Forcing someone to accept another paradigm is doomed to failure and could strain or even end friendships, thus creating low frequency energy associations. Instead, it's important to love all for who they are and meditate on their liberation.

When a person is ready to receive the truth, we will know.

Choosing Our Habits Wisely

Habits can be good or bad, but the nature of a habit is such that it is an automatic "invisible function" that we do every day. As such, it is ignored by our "physical consciousness."

Attention to what a habit is and what it is not, therefore, is a necessary prelude to success in the quest for attaining self-awareness and ultimate evolution. Such understanding helps us separate good habits from bad habits.

Good habits are those that lead to higher frequency existence and are ultimately supported by good like-minded people surrounding us. Good habits let us exist "within" the physical without being "of" the physical.

Bad habits keep our energies fixed within the low frequencies of the physical; therefore, they arrest our opportunities for evolution and perpetuate our need for incarnation.

Fulfilling Commitments

Completing our commitments with joy in our hearts is important. If we have committed to do something by a certain time and/or degree to or for anyone or anything or even ourselves, we must follow through and deliver what we have committed to do.

To not deliver our commitments is to relinquish responsibility for our thoughts, our intentions, our actions and our evolution. To not deliver our commitments makes that invisible commitment stay in the lower frequencies, thus, arresting our evolution.

Exercising Care

To gain high frequencies, it is imperative for us to be caring in all circumstances. For example, we must do the following:

- Care about what we do;
- Care about what we say;
- Care about what we eat;
- Care about what we drink;
- Care about what we breathe;
- Care about how we exercise;
- Care about how we help;
- Care about how we feel;
- Care about our relationships;
- Care about how others feel;
- Care about our physical education;
- Care about our spiritual education;
- Care about those we love;

- Care about those we don't love & love them, too!
- Care about our home;
- Care about our friends;
- Care about our country;
- Care about our planet;
- Care about our universe;
- Care about our relationship with God; and
- Care about **EVERYONE** and **EVERYTHING**

because God cares about US!

Being Mindful

Being mindful about what we say and do is imperative. We must do everything we can to ensure that whatever we say or do is constructive and not destructive, creative and not unimaginative, positive and not negative. Being mindful will help us make a difference.

Seeing the Light in All

If we see the light in everyone, then everybody will see the light in us. By illustrating that we see the light in everyone and everything, we also illustrate that we see the good in everyone and everything.

Illustrating that we see the light in everyone is a most positive step, for it is an addictive quality that breaks down barriers.

Following Source Entity's Ten Commandments

1. **Covet not another's property**. Why would we want to covet the property of another, especially if the means by which we live could not support it? Living the best we can by the means we have at hand and being

content, as well as remembering we are doing the best we can with what we have and the situation we find yourself in will bring us peace. Also, it helps to remember that whatever we own is only transient because this ownership is no longer ours when our physical body passes away.

2. **Covet not another's spouse.** The reason we are with our current spouse could be because we have worked together before or because we have some issues to work out together now for mutual evolution. This is an interesting commandment, for it is often the root cause of so much karmic energy. Of course, it means anybody else's spouse other than our own.

3. **Do unto others as they do unto you.** Why do we pain ourselves so much by trying to get back at others for what they do to us? It is not a creative use of our energies. We must try to put ourselves in their position, understand their issues and give them our help and love whenever we can—even if we just don't like them. Assisting them will be a big help for them, especially if they receive it from someone whom they consider to be their enemy or adversary. Maybe if we see the good in them, they will, too. If we don't, we create frustration and karma when we should be in acceptance and move on with love in our heart.

4. **Help others less able than ourselves.** This is a fundamental rule, for it is the one that has the most opportunities attached to it to help us evolve. The point here is that we should give help to those who need it when the opportunity presents itself. We must

remember we are all from the same spirit, the same Source. Why be selfish with our good health? Sharing it with others now opens the door for others to share theirs with us when our time comes to be less able— thus, coming full circle.

5. **Help others less fortunate than yourself.** As with #4 this is fundamental. Whereas #4 is aligned to the physical aspects of the human condition, this rule is closer to the situation that others find themselves in. Again, we are reminded to help others when the opportunity presents itself. The help can be as benign as shopping for them, servicing their car or buying them a meal when they need it.

6. **The universe is yours forever.** Why do we get hung up on ownership of physical things when the whole universe is ours for the taking when we take the time to realize it and work with it. As humanity we are hung up on ownership of the Earth, but no one owns the Earth. It is an entity in its own right. Once we realize that, we are able to go anywhere at any time and enjoy the universe and the earth in its entirety, so why would we want to pin ourselves down to a small section of it? Ownership of land and other physical things is okay as a comfort blanket, but in real terms when we are fully awakened to the reality that is around us, we really don't need to own or link ourselves to anything.

7. **Worship not graven idols.** This is relatively easy to follow in this day and age, for there is a greater level of understanding than there was a couple of thousand years ago. In essence this also works for churches as

well, for they are a larger version of the graven idol. Why worship the physical when we can meditate upon gaining access to the energetic/spiritual? The initial use of an idol was to give the initiate (a student of the truth, real truth!) something to focus upon when engaging in deep meditation. It has since been taken completely out of context and is no longer a requirement in today's society.

8. **Honor your parents.** This is mainly due to the need to help our parents when their physical bodies decay to the point where they are no longer able to contribute to the community in the way they used to. This is especially relevant in the last few thousand years when the knowledge and command of the energies of the universe have been lost to most of those who are incarnate. The older generation has all the knowledge of the past to give us and our children. Without them we would not appreciate our roots and would lose the fundamentals. Without the fundamentals the house of knowledge is but a pack of cards arranged in the shape of a house. There have been many incarnate races that have been laid bare, exposed to the elements, and nowhere to go as a result of catastrophe because they no longer had sight of the basic fundamentals.

9. **Do not tell lies about your neighbor.** This is again another general issue that is a major opportunity to gain karmic energy and slow down our evolution by being dragged down the frequencies. Why would we want to tell lies anyway? If we have done something wrong, we must own up to it and accept that we are in an

opportunity to experience something else in the physical that will be of benefit later. This also covers the terrible habit of gossiping about someone to try to gain favor with others around us. Eventually this backfires and costs us more karmic energy than we originally accrued. Worse still, it also "costs" those we gossiped about (unless they are more highly evolved) as they generally will want to "get one back" on us, which invokes karmic energy.

10. **Steal not from your neighbor.** Why steal at all? This is not necessary as what we have with us is all that we need to experience life in the physical according to the plan we laid out. The Lord/we shall provide, and we do. Everything is provided to ensure that our "sortie" on Earth in the lower frequencies is maintained at its most optimal evolutionary condition. This is another way to gain massive karmic energy because invariably we end up lying to cover ourselves if we steal.

Practicing Patience

Being patient with everyone, everything, and especially ourselves is an excellent practice. Adopting a calm and patient demeanor attracts higher frequency energies and high frequency friends.

When we are patient and calm, we provide an excellent example to others of how to live in the frantic world of the gross physical whilst avoiding lower frequency addictions associated with being restless.

Having No Expectation of Reward

Expectation can be considered the opposite function of desire, specifically when we expect a reward for being of service. Doing so also ties us into the low frequency desires of the physical and, therefore, delivers a level of karma.

Expectation is something to be avoided from a more personal perspective, especially when we "expect" a certain response or action from a friend or colleague.

Expecting nothing, we will gain two things:

1. Freedom from the karmic link that expectation gives us; and

2. Joy when a friend or colleague responds in the correct or most spiritually desirable way.

Anticipating Nothing

Anticipation is based upon expectation, therefore, it links us to a "desired" result. When we remove expectation, we will also remove anticipation, for the one creates the other.

When we remove both conditions from our minds, we negate the opportunity for us to enter into the "closed loop" of continuous cause and effect that creates the one or the other. Thus, it is wise for us to leave anticipation and expectation to their own devices.

Accepting Divine Providence in All Situations

When we anticipate an outcome, we paint a picture of what we desire, thus identifying that outcome as positive or a negative, based upon the outcome we anticipated.

Anticipation of an outcome is a human condition that ultimately links us to the physical.

When we are able to be in the "now," thereby removing the element of anticipation, we are working in acceptance that divine providence will prevail and bring the outcome that is the best for a particular situation.

Recognizing Situations as Opportunities for Evolution

Anticipation is a limiting thought process that is based upon our expectation of a desired outcome with desire being defined as "a condition of specific focus on the material."

Anticipation results from our expectation of a preferred outcome. In this case, our focus is on the outcome rather than the wider spiritual process that results in the outcome. Should the anticipated outcome not be that which we expected, then we become dissatisfied and/or are disappointed. When we feel this way, it is as a result of our working with the smaller "incarnate picture" rather than observing the result or outcome from the larger spiritual perspective. We must remember that no matter what the outcome, what is experienced is designed to help us evolve.

We should, therefore, accept situations presented in life as evolutionary opportunities rather than planning for certain "anticipated" outcomes and wasting time thinking about where and when the outcomes may happen and what they will be.

Accepting Frustration

Frustration is a product of desire turning into anticipation and expectation. It is based upon our inability to wait for that which will come with divine providence at the correct juncture in our incarnate existence.

Frustration is also borne from our inability to succeed in our plans. When we do this, it is the result of our not adapting to the learning opportunities that are presented to us to evolve;

instead, we choose to overlay these experiences with preferred outcomes instead of the actual outcomes.

Frustration can be avoided by expecting nothing whilst accepting everything and living in the product of the divine plan.

Being Impatient, a Predecessor to Frustration

Impatience is a precursor to frustration and its associated emotional responses. It is a product of our being in the physical whilst retaining an energetic memory of working within the energetic. Whilst in the energetic, we are able to affect changes instantaneously through pure intention that creates thought and later action based upon that thought.

In the low frequencies of the physical universe, this is not possible, but our memory of such function remains within us while incarnate—hence, our frustration when "things" do not happen. In this instance the antidote is to remain calm and wait patiently for the fruits of our work to come into fruition.

Impatience begins with its link to low frequency thoughts and desire for "instant gratification," a product of "modern times," where we simply "cannot wait" for this or that to occur. This pulls down our frequencies and negates the higher frequency thoughts of calmness and the joy of waiting for that which has been manifest to come into fruition. We deprive ourselves of wondering in awe at the processes that work behind the scenes to finalize that which has been manifested through intention, thought and action.

Feeling Dissatisfied and Impatient

We mustn't be impatient; we must watch out for impatience. It is a function of anticipative desire and is steeped in the expectation of that which may or may not happen.

Impatience is created when we are dissatisfied with that which we have, are, or expect to be, or from a temporal perspective, expect to be or have earlier.

As time does not exist in the energetic, impatience is, therefore, futile. We must trust that everything happens when it is supposed to happen to give us the correct level of experiential/learning content that will allow our flawless evolution to occur.

Experiencing Contentment as a Double-edged Sword

When we are content, we are ripe for working with the physical whilst being "in" the physical but not "of" the physical. We are not drawn to those lower frequency attractions of materialism that create a karmic link to the physical and arrest our personal ascension through the frequencies. We can soar above these lower frequencies and go ever onwards and upwards towards constant communion with our Creator.

However, if we are content with our spiritual progress and happy where we are, doing what we're doing and experiencing communion with spirit, we will never progress beyond that which is really just localized spirit. We will not reach the dizzying heights required to ensure constant communion with our Creator.

Offering Unconditional Love

Offering love—that is, unconditional love—is the most wonderful thing that we can give to one another. This should not be reserved for those that we know, love, trust, revere and respect, however. It should also be given to those that we "initially" don't know, fear, hate, loathe, dislike or distrust, for we are all part of the Source Entity. They are, therefore, part of us. Recognizing and experientially knowing this is a major step for us on the road to high frequency existence.

Sharing Kindness

When we are kind or offer kindness to anyone, whatever the circumstances, we take a step on our road to high frequency existence, for being kind is a prelude to unconditional love of one and all.

Perpetuating Karma

The universe does not run on karma. We as mankind create it through infatuation with the low frequencies associated with the physical. Why do we perpetuate that which does not naturally exist?

Evading a Competitive Mindset

We must avoid being in competition with others on all levels, including spiritual levels. Competition occurs when we are enticed into trying to become like someone else—someone who seems to have spiritual skills or abilities that we feel we lack and desire to have. We see this person as being better than we are and strive to become better than this individual is.

In circumstances like this, we forget that we are individual beings on our own paths. As such, we should and must concentrate on what we are doing in our own way and not try to be equal to or better than those around us. We need to just be ourselves and evolve by our own work in our own perfection and in our own time.

Being Complacent About Complacency

Complacency is the right hand man of karma. It waits for us when we feel that we have addressed all the spiritual issues that we need to work on and now need to do no more.

When we are convinced that the work is done, we are actually just about to start, for the task of working towards God and perfection is a lifetime's work, requiring constant diligence, introspection and re-calibration of spiritual achievement.

Accepting Everything

Resistance to that which happens in life that we consider to be sub-optimal is resistance to learning from those opportunities presented to us as lessons in how to disassociate ourselves from certain events—those events borne in physicality.

Our acceptance neutralizes resistance and negates our need to re-experience that which is experienced but resisted. When we neutralize resistance, acceptance can and does remove the opportunity for the karmic influence that resistance introduces.

Learning by Observation

When we observe those around us who are not aware of the greater reality, we often note how they work for the good of themselves and not for the good of everyone else and their Creator.

Although we will not be able to change them, they "gift" us a constant reminder of what we could become if we let ourselves slip back into the belief that physical existence is the only reality.

With this in mind, we will continue to work hard at being of service, meditating on our Creator, and experiencing the greater reality.

Comparing Ourselves with Others

We must avoid comparing ourselves with others. Once we embark upon the road of comparison with our friends, relatives, neighbors and peers, we run the risk of becoming dissatisfied with ourselves and our "transient" Earthly possessions.

Dissatisfaction is an insidious link to physical existence and one that demands us to be vigilant.

Living as Transient Custodians

It's imperative for us to remember that we are only custodians of that which we have around us whilst in the physical. We never actually own anything. Instead, we are only given the opportunity to work with, live with, and maintain that which we buy for the period of time we are incarnate.

Disconnecting the Physical from the Energetic Self

Physical pain is a constant reminder that we are in a physical vehicle that is limited by the thought processes of being incarnate.

"Limited" and "thought" are the operative words here for when we are not "limited" by the "thought constraints" of being in physical form and are able to work with the greater reality of being "in" the physical but not "of" the physical, then we realize that the physical form is a transient condition. As such, it is used for transitory moments of experience whilst we are in the lower frequencies that are associated with the physical universe.

When we realize—truly realize to the core of our being—this truth, we are able to disconnect our physical selves from our energetic selves and thus remove our mental link to the lower frequencies. In this way, by disconnecting our energetic selves from the function of pain in the physical vehicle we inhabit, we can live a pain-free physical existence and negate the karmic link in the process.

Such mastery of the physical requires dedicated, continuous, unwavering, focused, robust and intention-based thought 24 hours a day 7 days a week.

Being Vigilant of Addictive Sensations

Physical pain is a constant reminder that we are in a physical vehicle. Likewise, sexual sensations and other bodily addictions are also a reminder that we are limited by the thought/experience processes of the vehicle we are incarnated within.

Clearly some of the sensations we feel whilst incarnate are a joy to experience. Some, like sexual sensations, can be addictive. Others, such as touch, taste, smell and sight are sensations that are limited to our being incarnate. In the energetic we are above these sensations and, therefore, not affected by their potential additive qualities. In our need to be incarnate to aid our evolutionary commitment, we subsequently experience multiple sensations on a daily basis, some of which are a link to the low frequencies of the physical. We must be vigilant of sensations, for they can be insidious in their addictive qualities.

Using Desire with Care

It's important for us to be aware of our desires, for they are a route to the lower frequencies. If our desires are relative to things of the physical, then they will anchor us to the physical. If our desire is to commune with our Creator, our Source Entity—God, then our desire will be a route towards the higher frequencies and bring positive karma to us.

Being in Debt

In our earthly incarnate form, we must avoid indebtedness to anyone and anything either financially, materially, or in any other form. Debt is a control factor that leaves us under the control of the debtor. Debt of any kind links us to the physical. It ties us into the commitment of paying back the debt with interest, thereby compounding the debt and creating low frequency thoughts, such as resentment and anger, towards the debtor.

We should only have and recognize one debt, the one we all sign up to experience during our incarnation. We agree to experience, learn, evolve and share this evolutionary content, this debt of creation, with our Creator whilst maintaining this evolutionary content ourselves. This is not a physical debt, linking us to the low frequencies of the physical; instead, it is a debt of pleasure, of joy, of delight, of love, and of desire to help our Creator evolve by our individual efforts.

In this instance the best way for us to move forward is not to protect ourselves from the low energies associated with such thoughts but more to be in acceptance that we have placed ourselves in that position. We can, therefore, elevate our frequencies when we recognize the opportunity for personal growth from such a situation. We then work in joy at the prospect of paying back with interest that which is owed as a thank you to the debtor for helping us out when required. We do this without resenting ourselves for being in the situation or for the debtor charging interest—thereby, we break a karmic link.

Feeling Betrayal

Betrayal is an emotion we feel when our expectations of reward and recognition are not manifested. Indeed, betrayal is even more profound when we work for another, and the fruits of our hard work and the recognition we seek or expect is claimed by another. Betrayal can and ultimately does cause resentment, especially if we do not recognize and neutralize it by seeking higher advice or accessing higher knowledge on the need and requirement of the betrayer to commit the act of betrayal.

When we are betrayed in some way, we must use that opportunity as a chance to gain evolutionary content. It is important for us to take the position of the "observer self" and look at the reasons for the betrayer's need to deceive us. We have the opportunity to take true pity on this individual and freely give that which was taken without asking. When we do this, we re-direct the energies of betrayal to the energies of being in service—in service to the betrayer. We can then love this person and be in total and instantaneous forgiveness because this individual has given us the opportunity to take the function of betrayal and use it to increase our personal frequencies by acknowledging this as a chance to add to our growth experiences so we can learn and evolve instead of projecting anger, hatred and/or resentment at the betrayer.

Accepting Rather Than Resenting

Resentment, a particularly low frequency response, is a function of betrayal, expectation, personal comparison, and non-acceptance. Although it is a secondary function, caused by those other low frequency responses just noted, it masks the primary reasons for its existence and, therefore, masks its existence per se. When we are locked in the downward spiral of resentment, we place ourselves in the "poor me" and "why them" category of individual thought processes.

The antidote to resentment is our total acceptance of that which caused the primary function to come into existence. This is achieved by our using the detached "observer self" function, which allows us to recognize the processes and events that led us to be in this mental condition. In so doing, we should then forgive ourselves for taking such a route and forgive, accept and love those whose personal positions we have observed and considered to be better than our own. Even if they do appear to receive something for nothing and always be in the right place at the right time, we need to recognize that this is what they have agreed to experience whilst in the low frequencies of the physical universe, and this will enable them to experience, learn and evolve as all other incarnates do—in their own way.

Refusing to Ignore a Request for Help

Have you ever noticed that sometimes we ignore a fellow incarnate that needs help? We do this in myriad situations as we move quickly past the person in need lest we become involved, such as a beggar in the street, someone in a car accident, or a person in an abusive situation. After we've done this, we feel ill at ease. This is the feeling of energy being sent from the person "in need" to us, requesting our help and being ignored. This causes disharmony. If we get the feeling that we SHOULD help another, then we MUST help.

The discomfort felt in ignoring the request for help is also an indication that there is a need to help, based upon a pre-incarnation commitment between the person in need and us to work with each other. Notice how the common thought, "I should have helped there—but I didn't" lingers for a long time.

This is our opportunity to turn back and be the help that is requested.

It's also wise to remember that this may be an opportunity for clearing karma. Ignoring that feeling may create more karma or re-enforce the existing karmic link. Why take that risk when we can help the person and go home with a song in our heart?

Tuning into Others

When we "tune in" to the greater reality of others who need help, we gain a higher level of understanding and ultimately validate their needs or not as the case may be, for our help—our service.

If we "tune in" and feel that it is not necessary for *us* to be their liberator—and this is *not* a "way out" of being of service—then we can move on because there is no karmic link between us. However, we must ensure that the "tuning in" takes into account the possibility of creating karma—even if no karmic link was initially apparent.

Just because there is no link between us and someone else, it does not mean that a link cannot be created through neglecting the opportunity to be of service.

Those who request help but do not need it run the risk of creating their own karma—hence, the need for us to "tune in" first. In this instance when we gracefully decline helping the individuals, we are helping to ensure that they do not accrue karma linked to us through false requests. Thus it is that we are being of greater service in this instance.

Taking One Day at a Time

What if we were to start every day as if it was a new day, as if it was our first day on earth? We would have no troubles, we would have no enemies, we would have no worries, and we would have no concerns.

What if we considered that those things we have to do are a joy to do, that they are a challenge to be enjoyed, that those whom we meet are also a joy to meet for it is the first time we have met them, and it is the first time they have met us? We could ask what we could do for them without the need for reward.

What if we considered that the area we exist within is a joy to be in, an opportunity for improvement, an opportunity for positivity, and we could be in the now and work in the now?

In this state of mind we have no prejudices, no preconceptions, no fears, no insurmountable actions that are impossible to complete—just the joy of being here, of being able to participate and be of service. We are at peace.

Respecting Our Environment and Ourselves

When we respect our environment, the land, the trees, the sea and the animals, we respect ourselves.

Living in respect ensures that we are living in a higher frequency than that into which we incarnated.

When we recognize that we are all one with our fellow incarnates and with our Creator, our Source Entity, our God, then we should also realize that we are one with the rest of our Source's creations. This includes the multiverse, the physical universe, the galaxies and planets, the nebulae and stars, the earth, and its flora and fauna. In recognizing this, we will naturally respect everything in accord with how we treat ourselves—with respect, with kindness, with love, with wisdom and with oneness.

Being a Good Spiritual Example

When we ignore the needs of our siblings or children in terms of providing love, care, and wisdom, it is similar to ignoring our "self." Moreover, in terms of providing a spiritual education when our children or younger siblings are at their most impressionable, if we ignore them, it is tantamount to actively "denying" them the opportunity to receive a chance to better themselves early in their incarnation. They may then drift into "habits" within the material world that result in the accumulation of lower frequency existence.

We must not force such teachings but rather teach by example. A child that is surrounded by individuals of "good" spiritual habits will naturally accrue these habits, allowing them to survive exposure to bad habits and maintain their good habits. However, a child surrounded by individuals with bad habits will generally not be affected by exposure to good habits because of the intoxicating effect of those lower frequency bad habits.

When we ignore opportunities to demonstrate to children how to live and exist in a high frequency manner in a material world, we deny them a much needed spiritual education. This is a double-edged karmic sword. If we effectively expose them to intoxicating low frequencies or karma that results from our

50

promotion of or non-correction of their bad habits, we also expose ourselves to lower frequency thought processes through not caring or loving them enough. Ultimately, we create karma for ourselves as well.

Being True to Ourselves

Being true to ourselves should not be avoided, specifically when we are under external pressure to change.

When we are forced to be that which we are not in order to fit into another's paradigm, we are fulfilling the requirements of the other rather than ourselves. Serving the requirements of the self is just as important as serving the requirements of another, but not if it's to the detriment of the self.

We must stay true to our own beliefs, ethos, plans and personality even when others try to make us into something that we are not. This will insure that we work with them from the highest level. When we work from the level of truth and integrity, we negate the opportunity for exposure to and participation in low frequency activities whilst also being of service.

Eradicating Self-Doubt

Self-doubt is an important aspect of karma to recognize and is even more important for us to remove from our experiential vocabulary.

Doubt is a function of our remaining in a low frequency existence, being in the physical, and having limiting thoughts. These limiting thoughts are programmed into us the moment we incarnate, ensuring we work within certain guidelines and rules that deny us our heritage and our remembrance that we are an aspect of the divine—incarnate.

As an incarnate aspect of the divine, we are unlimited in this respect and when we recognize this fact, self-doubt dissolves and is unknown.

Limiting Thoughts

Limiting thoughts are a function of self-doubt, low self-esteem and a "frustrated" low frequency existence. The frustration is a function of the underlying knowledge that we can and should be capable of a higher level of existence. The limitations to our thoughts can be a product of our inability to think at a level above that which we are currently experiencing. It may also be the result of our being immersed in the low frequency thoughts surrounding others of a low frequency existence that we may "naturally" gravitate toward in order to create a feeling of oneness or togetherness.

Instead, it is essential that we surround ourselves with those people who are always pushing the boundaries of their experiences through unlimited spiritually aware thoughts. Doing so will and does result in our creating higher thoughts of unlimited content and thus raising our frequencies.

Attracting Lower Frequencies Through Jealousy

Jealousy is a rather invisible method of attracting the lower frequencies as it acts in several ways:

Firstly, we can be jealous about what another "owns." When we desire the possession of others, we create an association with the physical.

Secondly, we can be jealous about what someone has "made" of himself in this physical existence. When we do this, we create a link to the lower frequencies in an indirect method by desiring to be that which someone "is."

Thirdly, both of these jealousy-based methods of attracting lower frequencies are augmented by the inevitable self-generated competition we have with those who have that which we desire.

Maintaining a Healthy Physical Body

It's imperative that we look after our physical bodies. We must keep them well-exercised, well-nourished, well-hydrated and well-rested—both mentally and physically.

Although attractions to the lower frequencies of the physical are normally attributed to the actions resulting from dysfunctional thought processes that cause the addictions and habits that anchor us to these low frequencies, a poorly maintained physical vehicle can act as an attraction with equal effectiveness. This is due to the mental focus we have on the aches and pains, tiredness, slowness, and a lack of power if we are overweight and unfit. Ultimately, this results in mental and physical lethargy and a feeling of "giving up" because it's TOO HARD TO CHANGE!

Like attracts like, and if we are in the doldrums of the lower frequencies of the physical, then we will attract similar energies and the people associated with them.

And so it is that we must look after our bodies and stay bright and healthy as a result—thus, we create positive "high frequency" thought processes.

When we attract positive thoughts and high frequency responses, we will attract individuals of "like-minded thoughts." In turn, we will boost our frequencies, sever any attachments to low frequency functionality, and avoid karma.

Walking Our "Good Living" Talk

When we put into practice the theory of good living, we avoid negative karma. Thus, we can enjoy the reality of living this way, for we are breaking the karmic cycle.

Examining Oneness

Since all are one, we are reminded of that oneness when we associate with like-minded individuals who are working together in "metaconcert" for a single focused cause for the good of all. An example of doing this is a group meditation that focuses on sending love and light and remembrance to all that is as opposed to a group meditation focused on potential individualized gain.

False oneness is achieved via association of like-minded individuals working together to be part of the crowd in order to not be left out. This is oneness for the ultimate benefit of self and is a function of being in the physical.

Being Beholding to Another

Another way for us to avoid attaining karma is to avoid being "in beholding" to another in any way, shape, or form offered outside of "service." This could take the form of finances, favors, assistance, or direction.

When we are held "in beholding" to someone who gives us help outside of "service," that individual/"helper" gains control over us, the receivers of the help. Thus that person is able to hold us in ransom until we render a "certain" and usually "unknown" level of help in return.

The most difficult type of help to repay that is given outside of "service" is "favor" or "assistance" that leads to or provides significant benefit to us as recipients. This can result in our being "in beholding" to that individual for the rest of our incarnate existence with our repeatedly receiving reminders of the level of help given us in the past. In this way we are kept under control and in misery.

Thus, the only way we should give help is in "service" and receive help when the helper is providing us help under the pretext of being in service to us. This ensures that we are not "in beholding" to the helper, nor is the helper "in beholding" to us. Both are free to exist without the need to "give" in return.

Creating Self-Generated Karma

The ego is our "on-board" method of creating self-generated karma. We must beware of the ego and avoid its ways of creating karma while we are working within the physical environment. This includes working with those who are also incarnate.

Our ego was created during our incarnation process and is a transient condition that dissolves when this incarnation ends. As such, our ego does its best to perpetuate its own existence in ignorance of the fact that it cannot ultimately curtail its inevitable demise. In its ignorance, however, it perpetuates itself by luring us into a false sense of innocence that makes us negate its existence by attracting us to materialistic thoughts, actions and habits that make us "feel good" about our "self" through falsehoods. We must be vigilant and notice the conditions that make us "feel good" so we are not misled by the ego.

Some of these are position, status, appearance, belongings, influence and credibility with others. Clearly we generate some of these through "good living" as well whilst also being aware of karma; however, this can only be achieved if they are generated outside of ego's influence and are received in humility.

Being in Fear

Without doubt, fear is a low frequency emotion. We can be in fear of something without even recognizing it as fear or, indeed, a low frequency emotion per se. While incarnate, we often focus on that associated with our physical existence rather than remembering that we are very high frequency energetic entities momentarily incarnating in physical forms for evolutionary purposes.

As we become absorbed by fear, we are attracted to the lower frequencies by default. As such, our evolutionary progression is held back until we recognize and are able to resolve our attachment to fear and its low frequency energy. We can only achieve this by dedicated meditation on attaining full and direct communion with our Creator. This will lead us to recognition of our divinity, oneness with our Creator, and subsequent infinite longevity or immortality as an individualized unit of our Creator God.

Generating Karma Due to Boredom

From an evolutionary perspective when we create self-generated karma, it is like shooting ourselves in the foot. Self-generated karma, in essence, encompasses everything that is identified in this guide. Much of our karmic debt is a result of being "drawn into" various different situations by others, such as gossip, blame, crime, etc.; however, we can also create karma whilst totally isolated, both in location and in interactions with others.

Self-generated karma is, therefore, created by the attraction to and intoxication of low frequency thoughts, activities and habits. This happens when we are in a state of boredom and is created by the ego's need to maintain control of the so-called "conscious self." In this instance, the antidote is for us to use the time available (free time that results in boredom), to meditate on "just being" or contacting our Creator God, thereby using spare time in a most productive way.

Avoiding Coercion

Coercion is generated by persuading others to do our bidding rather than doing things ourselves. It is a practice we must shun at all costs if we are to avoid karma. Whereas persuasion is based upon our presentation of compelling evidence to encourage individuals to change the direction of their thought processes, coercion is insidious because it is brought into play to support the demands of the coercer through devious means, like threats to an individual's business or social position, family, and/or person or is favor-based.

To avoid karma resulting from the use of coercion, we must observe the methods we use to negotiate when negotiation is required. We must ensure that we employ only pure thoughts and true evidence in the negotiation process and not personality- and/or position-based persuasion or coercion.

If someone requests or we see that someone needs a favor, we should freely give it "in service" and not as a means of coercion.

Apportioning Blame on Others

If we apportion blame on another as a disguise for our shortcomings, we are disowning our actions and the results of those actions. Moreover, if we accept the accolades of success in tandem with apportioning blame to others, whether or not they are responsible, we are taking advantage of them in a most blatant and profiteering way. Thus, if we select so-called desired outcomes and discard undesired outcomes and then apportion the results of undesired outcomes upon those who may not be able to defend themselves, we are acting in a most irresponsible manner. In so doing, we are missing an opportunity for learning from that experience and evolving.

Apportioning blame is a double edged sword, for it not only adds karma but also negates the opportunity for evolutionary progression.

Using Others for Self-Gain

To use others for self-gain, a form of coercion, is a particularly effective way to accrue karma. It can be addictive, specifically if we are successful in the use of a particular individual and easily gain that which we desire. Through using others for self-gain, low frequency behavior is perpetuated and augmented as more and more success is achieved. Indeed, as an individual gains confidence in using others for self-gain, the use of others increases accordingly. Unfortunately so does the attraction to low frequency behavior. Additionally, because the level of confidence derived through expected success and improved coercive skill increases, there is further temptation to "use" others to the point of its becoming normal behavior for that individual.

The antidote is wonderfully simple in this instance. It is applied by doing ourselves that which we would use others to do. Thus, we achieve that which we gain through "our own hard work" and can justify the pleasures, satisfaction, and accolades bestowed upon us, for we will have not received them off the backs of others.

Committing Crime

Crime of any sort creates karma. If we know what is right and what is wrong according to the law and choose to do wrong, we have created karma.

Although it is recognized in many spiritual circles that there is no right or wrong, no positive or negative, and that there is only experience, it is a very wise incarnate that knows that there are certain paths that we must take in order to maximize evolutionary opportunities whilst within the lower frequencies of the universe, the Earth plane. As incarnate entities, we must recognize that there is a need to reduce the number of incarnations necessary for us to ascend beyond the need for incarnation-based evolution.

Committing a crime in this instance is not only an effective way of creating karma, it is also an effective way to reduce and even stop our evolutionary growth. Stopping or reducing our evolutionary growth opportunities is, therefore, a crime in itself—one that perpetuates karma.

Causing Physical Harm

Knowingly and deliberately doing physical harm to our "human" incarnate vehicle is defiling the very temple that we reside within—even though our residence is on a temporary basis.

Knowingly and deliberately doing physical harm to another's "human" incarnate vehicle is not the behavior of an evolved individual and invokes tremendous karma and low frequency attachment, especially when the act of "doing harm" brings pleasure.

Clearly we can and do have accidents when embarking upon experiential work as incarnates, and this is accepted. It is accepted because it is the "experiential content," the learning and subsequent evolutionary aspect of experience that results from accidental damage of our human vehicle, for this is ultimately part of our life plan.

Deliberately damaging the incarnate vehicle in some way to perpetuate its existence in general, such as with amputation, surgery, etc., is acceptable though. This is because the reasons for such actions are understood and recognized as part of the plan.

The antidote in all instances is to respect, maintain and nurture the human vehicle and recognize its true worth, importance and longevity. In this way we also respect the "vehicles" of others whilst also recognizing the necessity for the evolutionary growth of the incumbent spirits.

Harming an Animal Body

As with the incarnate human vehicle, knowingly and deliberately doing physical harm to an "animal" incarnate vehicle is not the behavior of an evolved "incarnate" individual and invokes tremendous karma and low frequency attachment. This is especially true when the act of doing harm brings pleasure.

We should recognize that spirits that incarnate as animals are very special gifts to us at this level of frequency, for they provide much needed unconditional love and company.

Although not the same energetically as those who incarnate in the human vehicle, animal spirits are also on the evolutionary ladder and respond positively in this respect from human love, care, and happiness. They are also individualized units of our Source Entity, our God.

In many cases animal spirits take on heavy burdens for us in our daily striving for survival in the physical universe, including being an essential component of the ecosphere. As such, the animal incarnate vehicle must be respected and maintained in the same fashion as we look after our own human incarnate vehicles.

We invoke the antidote to accruing low frequency energy when we recognize the true nature of animals as being "one with God" and, therefore, created in equality with our energetic selves. In essence, however, they have a higher level of purity when incarnate, for they are fully aware of the fact that they in most cases are dependent upon incarnate mankind's good will for their evolutionary progress. This level of purity is something incarnate mankind should aspire to.

Harming Flora

Knowingly and deliberately doing physical harm to a tree, plant or vegetable is an act of violence against an aspect of our physical environment, nature, and, therefore, our Creator, The Source Entity. Committing flora-related violence, therefore, creates flora-related karma.

Avoiding Karma

Although perceived by incarnate humanity as a lower life form, the kingdom of flora is extremely important from both a gross physical and energetic perspective to the perpetuation of the environment that supports the human physical form.

Clearly we have the authority to use nature to feed, clothe and house us, and this is accepted as essential for our well-being. We incur flora-related karma when we abuse this authority for personal or corporate greed or misdirected desire and destroy or fail to maintain those aspects of nature that are available to help us perpetuate our incarnate vehicles.

It is just as important to clear flora-related karma as normally accrued karma because both are functions of low frequency actions.

The antidote in this instance is to be "in joy" of that flora which surrounds us. We must nurture it, tend to its needs, and maintain it whilst recognizing how we can maximize nature's potential for evolution, for it can and does evolve as we live in harmony with it.

Wasting Natural Resources

The minerals that we use to create metals, ceramics, fuels and other materials are a gift to us from the earth. The earth in its sentience recognizes that our incarnate "human" vehicles are the tools we use for accelerating our evolution, and, as such, it supports that which we do with its minerals provided we use them for a high frequency existence that results in an increase in evolutionary content.

When we abuse this gift through inappropriate mining, extraction and refinement techniques due to personal and corporate greed, the earth suffers as a result, and we gain "earth-based" karma.

Inappropriate mineral extraction causes an imbalance in the ecosphere that affects the stability of the earth's crust as well as its magnetic properties, atmosphere, and weather systems. This creates further imbalance and ultimately adversely affects incarnate mankind's ability to work with the earth and attract evolutionary content.

When we realize that the earth is our benefactor and work with her in a high frequency harmonious way, we help maximize Earth's evolutionary content and as a result, negate karmic links with the earth.

Making Comparisons

When we make comparisons of any sort, it breeds discontent within us that breeds further comparison that leads to minor depression. Minor depression is fueled by comparison-generated discontent which creates a descending spiral-based loop that leads to major depression. Such a downward spiral is extremely difficult for us to recognize within ourselves and is even more difficult to reverse.

However, comparison can also be used as an antidote or can even *negate* the potential start of this condition if we use it properly and with observational care. If done correctly, comparing where we *are* in lieu of where we *were* can provide a spiritual function. Therefore, by observing what we have personally attained and thus comparing *ourselves* with *ourselves*, we can create a level of contentment and happiness.

When we are happy and content with what we have achieved, it brings a warm glow to us that illuminates the darkness and raises our frequencies as a result. Thus, it creates an ascending spiral-based loop that results in enlightened function and repeated frequential ascension.

Complaining, a Low Frequency Intoxication

Complaining about our position, status, situation, lack of ability, lack of help, health, or even that we feel we have been given a raw deal in some way is a function of low frequency intoxication.

Low frequency intoxication is a karmic function that results in our being so engrossed with physical existence that we forget that we are here to experience, learn and evolve. It makes us forget that this existence is an illusion, a VERY temporary illusion at best.

We are "incarnate" here to experience low frequency thoughts and/or feelings and learn to be victorious over them and thus evolve in the process.

When we can adopt the very useful tool of the "observer self," we can identify the early occurrence of such thoughts and recognize them for what they are—signs of low frequency intoxication. When we recognize this, then we will be able to succeed in the face of low frequency adversity.

Needing to Be in Control

Being "in control" is like colluding with a false friend. Although control is useful in situations that require us to control ourselves and others, such as in emergencies or situations of crisis, it is detrimental outside those contexts. Control is detrimental when we apply it inappropriately to ourselves and/or a third party.

When we apply unnecessary control to ourselves during our everyday existence, we run the risk of missing those spontaneous responses required to support "out of the blue" opportunities for us to experience something new. These types of opportunities are usually examples of circumstances given to us by our spiritual guide/s and helpers because we either need to change or need a change. This is called "going with the flow," which cannot happen if we are too self-controlled or always need to be "in control." In this instance, our being in self-control limits our abilities to access higher frequency information and keeps us in the lower frequencies, which is a function of karma.

When we are in control of others (third parties), we are tempted to use those under our control for the benefit of ourselves and not for their benefit. Even though we feel justified or even delighted or joyful being in control, the feeling of justification/joy in this instance is that aspect of control that tells us it is a false friend—for we should not be joyful or able to justify being in control of others.

Comparing and Contrasting

Contrast is a little known and mostly ignored function of comparison. When we compare and contrast our situations in relation to others' situations, we judge the differences and draw conclusions about the acceptability of these differences. We do this in the light of our newly acquired "standard" of a potentially better situation for us to be in even though it might not be.

If, however, we were to use contrast as a means of establishing where we can help others who are less able to provide for themselves, then we could turn this potential opportunity for accruing low frequency karma into an opportunity to gain high frequency karma and the relative evolutionary content. This is specifically pertinent when we are looking to use "contrast" as a means of establishing what we can provide to a group of individuals whose living conditions are poor in contrast to our own.

In this instance we are activating the evolutionary content aligned with our being of service instead of falling down the slippery frequential slope of dissatisfaction with our current situation in contrast to a higher standard—one which may or may not be appropriate.

Attracting Positive Karma Via Joy

Experiencing joy in our incarnate life is touching the very nerve of high frequency existence.

When we "en-joy," we are "in-joy." When we are "in-joy," we are in tune with all things and all things are in tune with us. This feeling is a sign that we are experiencing the high frequencies of spirit whilst incarnate.

It is important for us to try to hold onto situations where we are "in-joy," remember them, and then take them and that feeling with us wherever we go. We build upon them by adding other times and situations where we were "in-joy." In this way, we create a complete picture of joy and what we enjoy.

When we know and seek that which brings joy and are in a continuous state of joy, we automatically raise our base frequencies. Doing so allows us to experience new joy, ever new joy every time we are in joy.

As we experience higher and ever higher frequencies, we negate the influence of lower frequencies, no matter how hard they try to bring us down. In this process we ascend from the influence of karma. In this way we become closer to our Creator and experience the ultimate joy of being one with God.

Being Happy

Happiness is a product of joy and is an visible example of a state of joyful existence, thinking and being.

Personal happiness is the long term effect of being "in joy" and bridges the gaps between joyful experiences. The "joy-happiness-joy-happiness-joy" cycle is a profoundly efficient way of increasing our frequencies, especially when the experience of joy and the subsequent production of happiness is the result of spiritual activity.

In this way we can accelerate our evolutionary content whilst enjoying the process of gaining evolution and being happy with the outcome and lasting effects of such gains.

In essence, when we have the "joy-happiness-joy-happiness-joy" cycle fully established, we are capable of ever new joy and ever new happiness without gaps or loss of associated frequency. As a result, we can and do increase our base frequencies and ascend in the process.

Being in True Love

Love is the true antidote for all karmic influences. When we are "in love," we are in peace and harmony with everything and everyone.

This is not love in the human sense but in the spiritual or energetic sense. Human love is based upon physical attraction whereas spiritual/energetic love is based upon an understanding and full appreciation of the interconnectedness of everything that "is."

When we experience "true love," we understand the underlying reasons for everything that happens around us. Everything that is done by everything and everyone has a purpose and a meaning. When this is recognized and understood as such, even so-called "wrong doing" is recognized as having a purpose. This purpose is our need to experience, learn from that experience, and subsequently gain evolutionary content.

Being in "true love" then allows us to be in complete understanding of the process of incarnate existence. It allows us to see the beauty in everything and everyone, forgive wrong-doings even before they happen, and have no enemies. It is then that we realize all are fellow incarnates who are striving to evolve in the way we are with everything being in divine order.

When we are in "true love," we bear no ill feelings, do nothing to attract low frequency thoughts, and help everything and everyone in all circumstances. In the process we do not incur karma.

Committing Suicide

Suicide is a method of gaining massive instant karma. Karma accrued as a result of suicide is gained in two ways:

Firstly, for terminally defiling the gift of the physical vehicle because these are in short supply in comparison with the huge number of energetic entities requesting incarnate existence; and...

Secondly, not as a result of the act of suicide but as a result of the association with the lower frequencies that resulted in the desire to commit the act of suicide.

In essence the first way of gaining suicide-based karma is a result of the second way.

Recognizing Instant Karma

If we create any kind of suffering for another person and then receive back that which we gave that person or if we receive it back from another person, this is an example of "instant karma" or "divine retribution."

It can be helpful to receive instant karma for two reasons: 1) we are not tied to the karmic cycle as a result of the delivery of that which incurred the instant karma because we receive an equal action in return; and 2) we are able to learn from the mistake and correct it very quickly if we are observant enough to recognize the situation as a function of instant karma.

Instant karma, also classified as divine retribution, occurs when an additional function is being performed that is invisible to the person who caused someone to suffer (the dealer of the suffering to another), the person who suffered from the incident caused by another (second party "sufferer"), and the third party "dealer" who returns that suffering to the individual who was initially hurt. This function is the underlying ability of the third party to settle up previous and similar karma with the first party, which then clears that particular karmic link.

As with all that we do when incarnate, this relies on a significant level of logistics being performed behind the spiritual scenes with our guides and helpers working hard to assist us and those with whom we interface so we can experience, learn, evolve, and clear karma along the way. This is, indeed, a divine method of clearing karma.

Choosing Our Friends

It is important for us to beware of false friends—those that steer us towards low frequency pleasures, such as physical sensations or any form of materialism or gossip, for they are only helping us gain an addiction to low frequency existence.

A true friend is one that works toward spiritual advancement and avoids anything that does not focus on that goal.

A true friend is one that looks for the very simple pleasures in incarnate existence, those gained through correct living and meditation on the greater reality instead of the instant gratification that physicality offers and demands from others.

Avoiding Attachment

Attachment in the human sense—that is, attachment to another person—is also a very effective way to remain in low frequency existence. In this instance, attachment is not love but the "need" to be near or within the "presence of" a certain individual or individual's physicality.

Attachment is, therefore, a form of materialism, but because it is relative to the need for "personal presence," it is not easily recognized as such.

Attachment affects both the "initiator" of the attachment and the "focus" of the attachment as a result of an energetic link between the two. Keeping the "initiator" and "focus" linked to the frequencies associated with their physicality, which is a karmic function, retards the ability of both "initiator" and "focus" to ascend the frequencies, thus, creating a karmic cycle.

Clearly we create attachments to loved ones during our incarnation, but we should not hold onto them and remain attached when they are in the process of finishing their incarnations, for this holds both the "initiator" and the "focus" in the lower frequencies.

We plan our exit from the physical in the way that maximizes our experiential and subsequent evolutionary opportunity within a known incarnate timeframe. Unfortunately, this may not be to the liking of the one who has initiated or created the attachment. In this instance, we must accept that the exit method is pre-chosen and, therefore, respect and honor it. It is the time to send them true "non-attached" love, cognizant that in not having or actively removing attachment, we are helping them evolve and not holding them back in the lower frequencies of the physical.

Being in Divine Love

Infatuation is a significantly stronger form of attachment. It is to be totally engrossed in the physicality of another to the point of almost perfect distraction. In this situation, we ignore our need to service the activities that we are responsible for, specifically when we are in the physical presence of the focus of our infatuation.

Infatuation can be and often is disguised by love. When we feel that we are in love and not in infatuation, we are blind to its damaging effects. The only antidote in this instance is to first and foremost be in divine love and not human love; in doing so, we transcend the attraction to the physical condition and remove the opportunity for attracting karma.

Neither attachment nor infatuation can be sustained when we are in divine love, for when we are in divine love, we are in tune with all things, and all things are in tune with us. When we are in divine love, we realize the transient state of the physical with all its attractions and addictions and are, therefore, unaffected by such low frequency lures.

Achieving Detachment

Detachment can be both a help and a hindrance when it comes to low frequency attraction.

If we detach ourselves from higher frequency existence as a result of some form of distraction that makes us think that the gross physical is "all there is," then we become entrapped and succumb to the low frequency stimuli offered by the gross physical environment. This unfortunate process results in "reality blindness" as we focus on all forms of materialism.

If we detach ourselves from the lower frequency distractions of the gross physical that occur on a regular basis, then we can maintain our high frequency existence whilst incarnate. We grow as we experience these distractions, recognize them, learn from them, and act correctly. Subsequently, we evolve as a result of their transient effect. Though the effect is transient, it is beneficial in this instance because we recognize what it is, a function of low frequency existence. It is an opportunity for us as incarnate entities to recognize that which affects us. When we "see, feel and know" the reason for its existence and take the correct path, we negate its influence and turn it into positive karma that allows us to ascend in frequency as a result.

Feeling Divine Love

Divine love is all around us. It pervades the multiverse and is, therefore, part of our very being.

However, if divine love pervades everything, then why is it not felt by everyone and everything all of the time?

The reason for our not being able to feel divine love is because we get engrossed in the day-to-day function of existence in the gross physical.

We are here to experience the minute details of incarnate life, but they are often such major distractions. If we are able to take a regular break from our day to day commitments and give time for meditation and appreciation of all that surrounds us, then we can link into the energies that are the basis of the gross physical universe and, therefore, the multiverse.

These energies were used by the Source in the creation of the multiverse by giving up part of Itself. The Source is divine love and loves everyone and everything It created. We are one with the Source, and the Source is one with us. WE ARE THE SOURCE, and we are, therefore, in love, divine love, all of the time.

All we have to do is recognize this by opening our hearts during meditation and accepting everything that is. This will allow us to see past the physical, link in with everyone and everything, and recognize that we are all one—all one in divine love.

Aligning Ourselves with Divine Knowledge

When we align ourselves with divine or cosmic knowledge, we remove ourselves from the inaccuracies presented by the lower frequencies of the physical universe. When we are in alignment with the divine, we see through the façade of the physical, viewing it for what it is: a mode of experience designed to accelerate our evolution through hardships.

When we are aligned to divine knowledge, we can work with the challenges that are presented to us in the full awareness of that which we are experiencing and why we are experiencing it at a particular juncture in our incarnate existence. This allows us to make the best of situations and negates our need to experience the same thing through lack of learning the "lesson" the first time around.

To become aligned with divine knowledge, we must be diligent in setting aside an un-negotiable time to meditate with an open heart and an empty mind. Doing so allows the greater reality of divine knowledge to overcome the transient "little reality" of personal knowledge we create whilst incarnate.

We can only become aligned to the divine knowledge through dedication to knowing the truth and devotion to the ways necessary to allow us to open the door to the truth. It's a lifetime's work, but it's more than worth it.

Accruing Retrospective Karma

Retrospective karma is based upon our being pulled back into discussions or arguments about that which occurred in the past or previous event spaces (times). When we are drawn into gossip about that which happened in the past, we are not only attracted to those low frequency existences based upon that event space but also those low frequency events that were in action in the previous event spaces leading up to the low frequencies. This results in a "total immersion-based" recollection of that experienced frequentially.

Thus, karma accrues in two ways: 1) that which we accrue currently; and 2) that which we accrue by living in the past—retrospectively.

We exist in event space, not time, and as such event space has no boundaries. Event space exists concurrently. As a result, all that is related to what we call time (past, present and future) exists simultaneously in different "spheres" of events in specific areas of space which pervade the multiverse and beyond. Because event space is always with us, it is easy for us to accrue karma retrospectively, and, many incarnates attract karma in this way.

The only antidote is for us to live in the moment and refuse to be drawn into discussions about previous bad events or what bad event could happen in the future, based upon current trends. To do this, we should offer thanks to the antagonists and bid them good day, seeking instead good spiritually aware company.

Existing in a Two-Year Sphere

As incarnate beings, we exist in a two-year sphere where we only relate to that which occurred in event spaces up to the previous twelve months and those event spaces which relate to our plans within the next/upcoming twelve months. When we exist in this way, we are in constant exposure to similar or the same experiences unless we are capable of applying the content from lessons learnt in previous and similar experiences.

It is only when we have an event that causes us to re-focus, such as an accident, health problem or employment issue, that we bring in events from previous "related" event spaces outside the two-year sphere to assist us in resolving the problem or introducing the processes required to re-focus. In these instances we exit the current physical reality and encompass the inclusive "greater reality" which includes past, present and future events. Future events are only available to those with certain evolutionary content and subsequent base frequential aspects to support clairvoyance, clairaudience, and clairsentience, etc.

Pulling in experiences from event spaces outside the two-year sphere is a clear advantage because then we are able to recognize opportunities for not making mistakes similar to those previously made and thus not incur cyclic karma. Thus the antidote is our ability to exist within the two-year sphere, living in the moment as much as possible while drawing upon experiences from events outside the two-year sphere as much as possible. Learning the lesson once and applying that learning to our current experiences is preferable to experiencing and dealing with that experience as if it was the first time.

Recognizing Previous Actions/Reactions

Cyclic karma repeats itself in a known cyclic fashion when we have not quite learnt a specific lesson well enough to ensure that our repeated exposure to it will result in our choosing the correct "educated" action. Its function is twofold: 1) to expose us to similar experiences that achieve the same karmic result if the original is not recognized, and 2) to check if we have learned the process that made the karmic link in the first place.

When we recognize the processes that result in same or similar experiences, then we can act to ensure that we make the correct response/s whenever we are exposed to these experiences. In this way, we break the cycle of cyclic karma.

In this instance the antidote is for us to be vigilant, looking out for that which repeats itself and noting how we respond. Our goal is to endeavor not to repeat the responses that resulted in our lesson not being fully learnt and the karmic link being repeated.

Avoiding Cyclic Karma

Downward spiraling karma is repetitive (cyclic) karma that results in a gradual but ever increasing attraction to lower frequency existence with additionally increasing severity. In this instance our accrued karma attracts more karma (lower frequencies) the more we ignore repeated learning opportunities and actively choose to avoid the corrective action necessary to arrest their development.

When we are caught in the clutches of downwardly spiraling karma, it is extremely difficult, if not impossible, for us to reverse the trend on our own—unless, of course, this is part of our life plan. In this instance we need to be in acceptance of the observations and comments of those around us who can see the downward spiral occurring and accept the help they offer us. This takes humility on our part, which is a difficult personal thought process for us to adopt when we are "in the middle" of the spiral. It also needs true "resilient" friends to be our helpers when we are stuck in this type of karma, for they will encounter many episodes of resistance where they are not thanked for their help.

Grieving

Grieving is an essential part of our experiential existence in the physical; however, if it is taken too far, it can become a trap of the physical leading to karma.

Grieving itself focuses on our personal losses which are augmented by the passage of a multitude of shared experiences based upon the physical presence of an individual.

Grieving brings us great sorrow, which is not a true reflection of the experiences we've enjoyed; therefore, it distorts and dominates the memories of the joys previously experienced.

Although it can be difficult, the antidote is to change the focus from the immediate loss and reflect on the years of joy experienced in the presence of the incarnate that has now departed the physical form and ascended back into the natural frequencies of domicile. We must not dwell in the past (previous event spaces), for this is another form of karma. Instead, it is wise to wistfully remember that our incarnate life together was such an adventure and plan the next.

Living in the Past

Living in the past is a trap of the physical leading to karma. It leads us to comparison, dissatisfaction, negative reflection and inability to be in the present. The objective of being in the present and not the past is for us to take that which was experienced in the past and use it to affect correct responses to challenges that are presented to us in the "now."

Saying that we could have done better when reflecting on actions we made in the past, based upon what we knew at the time or thinking/stating that "things" were better in the past, only creates dissatisfaction with our past performance. This creates a continuous regime of negative reflection.

We act and react based upon our experience and ability to deal with that presented to us. How we determine the "quality of an event" is how we deal with that presented to us using the tools of ability and prior experience. Accepting that how we reacted and acted was the best that we could have achieved in those circumstances is called "living in the now." When we recognize this, it negates our need to constantly refer to the past in comparison to the "near present" or "now." This then allows us to move forward in our evolutionary growth rather than turning that achieved into a function of karma, based upon physical performance.

This does not negate the need to learn from our mistakes, but it does negate the need to chastise ourselves when we spot our "mistakes" retrospectively.

Being Grateful

When we show gratitude for a good deed someone extends to us, it encourages further good deeds. We can extend gratitude when we personally receive a good deed, as well as when someone else receives one. Indeed, our expressing gratitude is a mark of recognition not only for the deed itself and its importance but also for the thoughtfulness of the giver in seeing our needs or those of others.

We must not, however, give false gratitude that merely acknowledges the deed for acknowledgement's sake, for this is as negative as giving no gratitude at all.

Simply appreciating that which has been done for us or others extends gratitude to that which has been done in a passive way. Passive gratitude is "received" energetically by the doer of the good deed, as well as subliminal encouragement.

The promotion of good deeds through gratitude is, therefore, an accelerant. There is a pattern here. The more encouragement we or others receive though truly given or received gratitude, the more we or others will do good deeds, eventually elevating ourselves to the level where good deeds are normal for us, and we will no longer need for recognition for them. At this point in our development, we will be in true service, avoiding karma in the process.

Being Mindful

Being mindful of how we function whilst incarnate is an excellent tool in our battle against accruing karma. Being mindful means that we give ourselves enough time to think about what our environment is, how we are being affected by it, how we are being affected by who and what is in our environment, and how we can efficiently deal with who and what is affecting us without creating low frequency attachments of any kind: transient, short, medium or long term.

In this instance, we as mindful incarnates can see all the possible links to low frequency or karma-generating responses or reactions so we can avoid them with ease and maximize their incarnate evolutionary potential at every opportunity. This is true even in adverse environments or conditions.

Gaining Mindful Appreciation

Appreciation through mindfulness is a very powerful way for us to tune into the functionality of the physical universe we exist within.

If we are mindful enough to see beyond our initial experience to observe the beauty in the interactive properties of what we are experiencing, then we can accept every experience and whatever it brings with an appreciation of the underlying evolutionary opportunities being presented to us and welcome them with open arms—thus avoiding karmic forces.

Observing the Details

When we show appreciation through mindfulness, it allows us to experience the minute details of physical existence. For example, we may observe the work behind the presentation of the foods we eat.

We can do this from so many perspectives, for example, seeing or thinking about the planting of a seed, the growing and nurturing of the vegetable, harvesting the crop, washing and preparing it for sale, delivering it from the farmer to the shop and then to our larder, and from our larder to the cooker and then noting all the work of the cook or chef to bring it to our plate. We note some or all the work done to get this food to us to taste and experience and the energy we gain, the zest we feel when energized by the food.

When we are appreciative through mindfulness and recognize the work required to deliver what we need in our everyday incarnate existence, we offer no negativity and are grateful for what we receive, irrespective of what it is. We give thanks and encouragement. Our doing so, promotes high frequency responses in the process and avoid the potential low frequency responses relating to karma.

Balancing Our Experiences

Experiences that we classify as bad or "sub-optimal," such as the loss of a loved one, the loss of a position of power/responsibility, an accident in our motor vehicle, or a paint can spilling on the carpet while decorating our home are all part of our undergoing a balanced set of experiences in the physical.

We expect good things to happen to us all of the time whilst incarnate and, as such, we tend to focus only on those things that we classify as good or "optimal." We ignore the importance of experiencing the so-called bad or "sub-optimal" situations. However, it is how we respond to these sub-optimal experiences in comparison to the optimal ones that dictates whether or not we are consumed by being "in" the experience.

When we experience optimal events and pay little or no attention to them, we are "part of them" but "not of them" unless, of course, the ego has a part to play in the optimal experience. When we experience sub-optimal events, we pay a lot of attention to them and become "of them" but not "part of them." In the latter, we forget the bigger picture that these experiences include, and the result is an unwilling attraction to the lower frequency responses associated with the experience through emotions, such as disappointment.

The antidote that is written several times throughout this guide is to stand back and see what the experience offers us as a lesson. We must take time to see what the correct response route is. Have we learned the lesson and gained the evolutionary content attributed to the experience? With this knowledge in mind, we can see the beauty and its timeliness in the experience and then rise above the opportunity for entrapment in the lower frequencies.

Smiling in Adversity

Smiling in the face of adversity is an excellent way for us to remain in a high frequency existence whilst we are incarnate. Smiling in the face of adversity means that we are not consumed by the lower frequencies of the adverse condition but are "in joy" at the opportunity of dealing with the challenge/s presented to us.

Remembering, the Key to Avoiding Karma

Remembrance, particularly of who and what we are and why we are here is the ultimate key for us to avoid karma.

Through diligent daily meditations, we as incarnate individuals can establish communion with the greater reality. Thus, we gain comfort that incarnate existence is but a transient part of our total existence and understand our part within it. This allows us to look deeper into "what is," which will allow untapped levels of our energetic memories to become accessible and thus in increase our levels of "knowing," which "is" a function of remembrance.

When we are in "remembrance," we know how to react in an optimal way to all experiences in all environments and navigate with ease through the maelstrom of opportunities for low frequency attachment—thus avoiding karma.

Source Entity's Words of Wisdom to Avoid Karma

In this section I have included a number of the Source Entity's "words of wisdom" that I felt should accompany the ways to avoid karma presented in this book. Each one has been specifically chosen because of the way it augments the guidance already given. Indeed, in terms of advice, each is more than capable of "standing on its own two feet," so to speak, which is why it is included.

When the Source uses the word "we," it is considering Itself as one with all of us—as us. As we experience, It experiences. As we learn, It learns. As we evolve, It evolves.

We must become our own gurus and stop to consider what is being presented to us via experiences and run a number of "what if" scenarios before we decide what to do. Then we choose the optimal response and record the result. If the response chosen was not the optimal response, we look at what made us choose that response in the first place and make a mental note not to repeat it in that scenario again.

When we learn from choosing certain responses and recording the outcomes mentally, we develop a database of known paths or processes to follow when we are confronted with a similar new experience. Thus we ensure we will have a successful response the next time and thereafter. In essence, when we learn the lessons and robustly apply that learning, we are not only good students but also good teachers, for the student and the teacher are one and the same.

The light within is the light without. Unless we are able to accept that our light is within, we will not shine without. When we accept the light within, we are in the knowledge that we are a beautiful being, one with our Creator, perfect in every way, and nothing outside us will extinguish this inner light.

The light of beauty is not only in the eye of the beholder, it is within our spiritual eye if we can behold it within ourselves.

The roads to God are many and varied, but whatever road we take, we must make it our own. We must be persistent and patient and not enticed by the road of another, which may seem faster but actually isn't.

If we are selfish, it is OK, provided we are only selfish in seeking the road towards communion with God.

When we are calm and adapt to change without apportioning blame, we possess the ticket to ascending with the ascension.

Avoiding Karma

Ascension is inevitable provided we continue questioning our reason for existence and thus maintain our desire to know why and how our universe was created.

Meditation is the ability to concentrate 100% on God, and as a result, to become aware of God's presence.

Fear is the barrier the ego uses to keep us from communion with God, as communion with God results in loss of ego.

Why fear that which we are part of? God loves us because we are part of God. Because we are part of God, we are loved by God and can experience God. However, God can only be experienced by looking inwards and being quiet and still.

In the search for oneness with God, we must first open the door of the heart. Only then will God step through the doorway.

Our reason to be is to awaken in God, know God, be one with God, and be God whilst incarnate—a simple task that we make so hard to achieve by succumbing to our physical desires.

Within silence there can be found God; within God there can be found silence—the silence of joy in knowing God.

Some choose to awaken comfortably. Some choose to awaken uncomfortably. Acceptance is the recipe for awakening comfortably; resistance creates discomfort.

That which is seen by the physical eye is but a microcosm of a microcosm of a microcosm. It is not the real reality, for the physical is a creation made by our Source Entity, our God, to allow us to experience the minute details of what has been created, the multiverse we exist within for the purpose of evolution. If we would open our eyes, we would see beyond the façade which separates it from the rest of creativity.

To open our eyes we must be fastidious in learning to meditate, to seek the truth, to renounce that which appears to be real, to be unwavering in our desire to be part of the greater reality, to avoid getting tied up in the theater of existence in the physical, to forgive and forget, to help without expectation, to exist in love and harmony—to "BE" that which we "ARE"—"ONE" with our "Creator."

Why should we settle for consciousness in the physical when we can commune with God and gain cosmic consciousness?

There is no separation. We are one with God, and God is one with us. Why seek externally that which is always within?

Why do we put off contacting God today in lieu of tomorrow when we can do it today and tomorrow and the day after . . . ?

God judges us by our actions, not words, so when we say we are going to meditate on God, we must DO IT! And be rewarded by communion with God and not the "thought" of communion with God.

Embrace that which is within—God!

Spiritual physics is the understanding of the existence of knowledge that is "beyond" knowledge.

Whilst we are in the physical, reality is, in essence, that which "we think we know" but ultimately "will know" when we translate back into the energetic.

It's wise to question ourselves on what reality is. It is not the mundane need to wake, work, eat, sleep and be better than someone else.

Forgiving is the biggest gift God has given us. It should be unconditional and instant.

egativity should be seen as an opportunity for creating positivity.

Avoiding Karma

To move into the multiverse whilst incarnate, we need to recognize the physical universe for what it is, and what it is not.

It "is not" the true reality; "it is" an opportunity for individual evolution.

It "is not" the be-all and end-all or the opportunity to be the dog that ate the dog; "it is" to be the dog that loved the dog and shared its scraps of food in equality.

The physical universe is nothing but a theater, a play we created, an opportunity for us to endeavor to remember our lines and our actions when we are faced with the experiences we have chosen. For this reason everything we do is within the play, a play manifested in the theater called Earth.

Avoiding Karma

We must be discerning in relation to our work and take onboard only that which resonates with us as truth. There is a lot of spiritual text that is written by the ego or is "band-waggoning" rather than coming from the source of truth. We must take onboard that which resonates with us as being correct.

Many teachers today present the same information in different ways. This is necessary because we are all at different levels of evolution and awakening. More importantly, we all learn in different ways of absorbing and experientially knowing. So what may be kindergarten spiritualism to one person may be high spiritualism to another. Ascension is, therefore, for all of us.

Seeking to understand where we are in comparison to another is not good practice, for it introduces jealousy or ego.

Dates are a great misnomer as we become confused when nothing discernible happens that can be attributed to the date. They can, however, be used as a milestone to indicate that we (collectively) should have reached a certain level of frequency.

We ARE ascending through the frequencies at a sustainable and robust pace, one that will allow us to have minor setbacks without affecting our overall process of ascension. The knife-edge ascension that most spiritualists desire is not optimal, nor is it sustainable because it is just as easy to descend as it is to ascend the frequencies. With a big jump, the drop can be just as big.

If we are all one, how can we be singular? If we are all singular, how can we be all one?

The answer is that we are all the collective totality of the entity we call God.

Physicality to Energetic/Super-Conscious Mind Equation

Physicality (incarnate self) minus the conscious mind minus the subconscious mind equals the super conscious or energetic mind.

Avoiding Karma

$$i.e., ((P - CM) - SM) = SC/EM$$

or

$$((Physicality - Conscious\ Mind) - Sub\ Conscious\ Mind) =$$
$$Super\ Conscious/Energetic\ Mind$$

About the Author

Guy Needler MBA, MSc, CEng, MIET, MCMA initially trained as a mechanical engineer and quickly progressed on to be a chartered electrical and electronics engineer. However, throughout this earthly training he was always aware of the greater reality being around him, catching glimpses of the worlds of spirit. This resulted in a period from his teenage to early twenties where he revelled in the spiritual texts of the day and meditated intensively. Being subsequently told by his guides to focus on his earthly contribution for a period he scaled this back the intensity of spiritual work until his late thirties where he was re-awakened to his spiritual roles. The next six years saw him gaining his Reiki Master and a four year commitment to learn energy and vibrational therapy techniques from Helen Stott, a direct student of the *Barbara Brennan School of Healing*[TM], which also included a personal development undertaking (including psychotherapy) as a course prerequisite using the *Pathwork*[TM] methodology described by Susan Thesenga with further methodologies by Donovan Thesenga, John and Eva Pierrakos. His training and experience in energy based therapies have resulted in him being a member of the Complementary Medical Association (MCMA).

Along with his healing abilities his spiritual associations include being able to channel information from spirit including constant contact with other entities within our multiverse and his higher self and guides. It is the channelling that has resulted in *The History of God, Beyond the Source* and is producing further work.

As a method of grounding Guy practises and teaches Aikido. He is a 5th Dan National Coach with 30 years experience and is currently working on the use of spiritual energy within the physical side of the art.

Guy welcomes questions on the subject of spiritual physics and who and what God is.

Website:

www.guystevenneedler.com

or email at beyondthesource@btinternet.com

Other Books By Ozark Mountain Publishing, Inc.

Dolores Cannon
Conversations with Nostradamus,
   Volume I, II, III
Jesus and the Essenes
They Walked with Jesus
Between Death and Life
A Soul Remembers Hiroshima
Keepers of the Garden.
The Legend of Starcrash
The Custodians
The Convoluted Universe - Book One,
   Two, Three, Four
Five Lives Remembered
The Three Waves of Volunteers and the
   New Earth
Stuart Wilson & Joanna Prentis
The Essenes - Children of the Light
Power of the Magdalene
Beyond Limitations
Atlantis and the New Consciousness
The Magdalene Version
O.T. Bonnett, M.D./Greg Satre
Reincarnation: The View from Eternity
What I Learned After Medical School
Why Healing Happens
M. Don Schorn
Elder Gods of Antiquity
Legacy of the Elder Gods
Gardens of the Elder Gods
Reincarnation...Stepping Stones of Life
Aron Abrahamsen
Holiday in Heaven
Out of the Archives – Earth Changes
Sherri Cortland
Windows of Opportunity
Raising Our Vibrations for the New Age
The Spiritual Toolbox
Michael Dennis
Morning Coffee with God
God's Many Mansions
Nikki Pattillo
Children of the Stars
A Spiritual Evolution
Rev. Grant H. Pealer
Worlds Beyond Death
A Funny Thing Happened on the Way to
   Heaven
Maiya & Geoff Gray-Cobb
Angels - The Guardians of Your Destiny
Maiya Gray-Cobb
Seeds of the Soul
Sture Lönnerstrand
I Have Lived Before
Arun & Sunanda Gandhi
The Forgotten Woman
Claire Doyle Beland
Luck Doesn't Happen by Chance

James H. Kent
Past Life Memories As A Confederate
   Soldier
Dorothy Leon
Is Jehovah An E.T
Justine Alessi & M. E. McMillan
Rebirth of the Oracle
Donald L. Hicks
The Divinity Factor
Christine Ramos, RN
A Journey Into Being
Mary Letorney
Discover The Universe Within You
Debra Rayburn
Let's Get Natural With Herbs
Jodi Felice
The Enchanted Garden
Susan Mack & Natalia Krawetz
My Teachers Wear Fur Coats
Ronald Chapman
Seeing True
Rev. Keith Bender
The Despiritualized Church
Vara Humphreys
The Science of Knowledge
Karen Peebles
The Other Side of Suicide
Antoinette Lee Howard
Journey Through Fear
Julia Hanson
Awakening To Your Creation
Irene Lucas
Thirty Miracles in Thirty Days
Mandeep Khera
Why?
Robert Winterhalter
The Healing Christ
James Wawro
Ask Your Inner Voice
Tom Arbino
You Were Destined to be Together
Maureen McGill & Nola Davis
Live From the Other Side
Anita Holmes
TWIDDERS
Walter Pullen
Evolution of the Spirit
Cinnamon Crow
Teen Oracle
Chakra Zodiac Healing Oracle
Jack Churchward
Lifting the Veil on the Lost Continent of
   Mu

For more information about any of the above titles, soon to be released titles,
or other items in our catalog, write or visit our website:
PO Box 754, Huntsville, AR 72740
www.ozarkmt.com

Other Books By Ozark Mountain Publishing, Inc.

For more information about any of the above titles, soon to be released titles,
or other items in our catalog, write or visit our website:
PO Box 754, Huntsville, AR 72740
www.ozarkmt.com